For Hunger

Margaret Ronda

saturnalia books

Distributed by University Press of New England
Hanover and London

Saturnalia Books
105 Woodside Rd.
Ardmore, PA 19003
info@saturnaliabooks.com

ISBN: 978-1-947817-99-9
Library of Congress Control Number: 2018949141

Book Design by Robin Vichnuch
Printing by Versa Press
Cover Art: Adriaen Coorte, "Four Apricots on a Stone Plinth"
Courtesy of the Rijksmuseum, Amsterdam

Author Photo: Tobias Menely

Distributed by:
University Press of New England
1 Court Street
Lebanon, NH 03766
800-421-1561

Thank you to the editors of these journals in which some of these poems originally appeared: *Aufgabe, Columbia Poetry Review, inter/rupture, Los Angeles Review of Books Quarterly Journal, Ostrich Review,* and *West Branch.* My gratitude to Henry Israeli and Christopher Salerno for your support of this book. Abiding thanks to my family, and to Gabrielle Calvocoressi, Julie Carr, Jessica Fisher, Ted Martin, Annie McClanahan, Evie Shockley, Carol Snow, Sasha Steensen, Brian Teare, Cathy Wagner, and Elizabeth Young. And to Tobias, for love.

*for Priscilla
and for Rowan*

Table of Contents

Can I eat
what you give me. I
have not earned it. Must
I think of everything

as earned.

—Robert Creeley, *For Love*

1

Nocturne

What comprised me, drew me in. The wind in the dark, in staccato.

When the neighbor's light burned out, darkness seared my body, its color glaring on the tongue.

A trespass on attention, like a knock at the pane.

From sleep, the boy calls out, there's a robber in my room!

But not the robber-girl, with her hundred pigeons and shiny knife, the robbers' greedy eyes. *'Tis gold, 'Tis gold!*

A word flinty and red at the core. You resemble the dark.

Is it the wind at the gate? Or only a hungry child sleeping in a story?

Sonnet

to catch a weather and mother it quiet
to cradle the gullfeather in an electric net
to cull from the spindle a dress of gold flax
to blacken the mouth of drowsy indolence
to resort at last to impossible measures
to rue the breath's frail-slurred murmur
to rescue blight from the ice-stunned orange
to patch up each almanac teary and worn
to bridle the jubilance of just-woken horses
to brew sweet tea for a blackguard called peace
to pare pixels into hammered stars
to wake a sundial from the hall of locked hours
to marry each countenance tender and iron
to wash the black dog clean of desire

The Hunger Patient

The oldest story: mother as aversion and desire, daughter as darker, dispossessed, as tender and tended to, as tether. The mother all symmetries, the daughter forged improvidently.

A borrowed dress, a forgery. Daughter a watcher, mother the impenetrable tower.

I wanted to eat all day. To become all body, to take the entire world in. Never have I been so famished. I devoured her untouched trays of food, cafeteria meals, chocolates and oranges the nurses would cadge. I refused nothing.

Read her nostalgic stories. The words on my tongue—*Once there were four children whose names were*—stale nourishment. Always she was tired, stoical, she wanted sleep, a stream of phrases to half-hear, or nothing. Held the plastic cup to her lips as she drank, wearily. Hours of her sleeping, oceanic suck and thrum. To be shelter and succor for one who wants not.

Favorite childhood tale: Marie in gold and Marie in tar. One is punished for one's earthly wants. Two girls asked, Were you born in a cabbage or a rose?

I grew in her unseen, a skinny shadow. At the verge of absence—"run and play" as she lifted me into the grass. And so I ran, borrowing her gait.

Three pills in a cup augured morning, glass of water mistrusting her fingers. I deadheaded the roses and weeded the hawksbeard.

The machine slipped inside her and found itself irresistable there.

I scraped away snail shells and trimmed the sedges. Flurry of nurses going silent in the jubilee garden, a row of sympathetic eyes. She says, I haven't seen myself for weeks. Another hour slumped in the tidied air. Her body was all mine, but her face was missing.

She often said she could feel Christ "just beyond her sight," dwelling in unseen corners. In my child's mind: a green shirt of wind. She called herself his "seeker and servant." She called him her "bread."

In the dream, she beheld a great tree, suffused with sunlight. "And we are the leaves."

One morning, a man knocked on her door, but she refused or was unable to answer.

Stripped now to animal humiliations. All body. Crushed birdskull curled in a white box. Little hermit sphinx with bloodied organ swinging above its head. Sallow cleanplucked hen. Gaunt and gutteral, moan and claw. Hated her sour breath, black sores on her mouth, fouled and rank. Her skin stitched haphazardly, spittle and heaving bile. Yet I did nurse her close to my breast, timorous beastie, o creaturely life.

I learned to mind it, ration it, lull it down. Hoarded it, hushed it, child now be still.

"The woman who wishes for a child white as snow and red as blood gets it."

The baby wants to be fed but the mother is sleeping. The baby needs a new language. And the mother, whose sleep is the central fact, whose breathing devours the room. In her sleep she erases all matter, refuses time and air and the mouth, laboring. Hush now.

To Labor

Is she is it to harden to yoke the bloodlit eyes to tarry

to suture each crack

to stalk and bind burrow and flag to gag the swarming mouth

labor to weave til rust til halved

to strive at the wheel to thrash the oiled rail

is it to soothe the blistered the burst

is she

to couple to heave and boil

to stanch in yarrow to grit on teeth

to bury wood and burn bone

to force to fetter

to fallow the rot to drag the thrown weight

to retract to recoil

is it is she

to measure to mind and mend

to maintain

hush suckle scrub

to shape to shell

to pitch and sway to beat and knead

to earn to learn to lose

labor to bear it forth phrase it

kill it will it be reborn

Seasonal Affective

Slept in redlit room. All rivery with wine. Air borrowed, ashiver. A
nearness, weekday milky tender and kissing. Rusty stain.

A golden coat in Le Marais. Stacks of oranges, radishes, squash,
intricately carved meats. Stone and strewn. How to say yes, more,
enough. Learning to bow in language's absence, passive in the face.
Schoolkids erupting colorful in sudden icy air.

Corner of Rue St. Denis, shattered car and the man with bleeding
hands. Stopping or not stopping. All traffic suspended under the sea.
Tea steeped too long, swampy as marriage.

A month, another autumn in a neighbor tongue. Floated in without
company on alley air. It's salty and full of fog, and the birds burned
off. Snapped the photo and disappeared. Light-fleeing days.

Days of novelty hedged with an older rain. The sink dripped a thousand times. She was living further into radiance, hair and skin eroded. Cells neoplastic. Said she was all circulation, all kinds of air colliding.

Fat with sleep. Industrial odor seeping from the grate. The tub too small for washing. Some kind of animal clawing at the roof. Sandalwood soap under nails.

The city from above only in dream. Skipped through agitated leaves of Les Halles, sad teenagers slouching on steps. She never spoke of dreams or memories or cities.

Hurtling zones with a slight electric crackle, her voice growing quiet, what unsaid, leaving.

Leavings, shops shuttered, crossed-off maps. Landless the sea swarms.

Train, tube, bus, another. Couple cackling, no words, the drunk with his duty-free whiskey.

Red cap and three sweaters for seawind. A suitcase with apples, lipstick, books on agricultural ruin. Always a war on, bomb in the market, rubble underground.

England in October, freezing rain and obsolete roses.

Storm blowing in, no one saw its expression. Small red room without shutters, pipes banging the heat through.

Through the window the sea rearranges itself. On the rocks a
slack seagull. Raining but not in her mind. Tide verging,
unwoven.

Sorry to leave the shore, she said.

Love at a distance, a newlywed song, lying on the green carpet
and the phone rings. Figs in the Paris market, hashish, the
pleasure-boat drownings.

Small neat kitchen with enormous windows, cookbooks teas pills
in a row. Shaken voice of BBC correspondent at the scene. Who
is responsible.

Her mind on the ocean.

The ocean's long sleep. Each dream leads to a different present. Chose the one where each city is a forgetting, a try-again-tomorrow. Back and forth on the Canebière, *porter emporter supporter.*

Out composing again, so hot this late, pastis and traffic. Rimbaud died here, a kind of licorice smell and freighters. Spoiled afternoon with debris.

Can't get a foothold. So much for consumption, unhappy fish dart in the atrium. Seasonless as California, each quartier hopeful and impenetrable, a new desire, artificial map's assembly. Port of the empire, *allons enfants de la Patrie,* here is where and there.

Easy and rough, a gang of shipwrecked kids. Minimal hour, sun and not. Wrong clothes for this voyeurism. Interior without hope, a meal eaten with strangers.

Together, apart, her voice always welling up, a shore of pure infrastructure, a callanque where a girl was lost for days.

For days an impatience with the question, legible tissue of cityscape too flimsy, the answer never yes or no. Motion is sleet in the virtual sky of Paris.

Nursing the solstice, winter horizontal, frozen heaves on.

Five seasons measured in scans and prognoses, a debt to burden home, it's how many months will she.

Sleep shifts, after a while, into another word.

The word for time and weather, the word for roses, for leaves, leavings. Yesterday fleeing further into radiance. Today heavier on homebound.

What is the opposite of travel?

Love, territory, darkness.

Book of Days

ice chips, nettle tea
nothing going through

cold in her mouth
then spits it into the plastic bowl

*

alone and eyes on fire
as the child
whose fur has gone matted and strange
washed in insect blood

I once was and am
a child

as the eye flinches
damage you can't unwill

*

growing very tired in her listening

she's a door open halfway

late daffodils and garish lilies gone brown
pollen dusting the floor
and the dogs panting
heaving blood
black liquid pools in plastic bag
breath in out in

*

blinked and wondered open in surprise

but as if through a screen

oh my eyes filling with fear or

this burden of sleep
which is the dream of older nights

now always with a color
in my eyes so unlike
what makes the sun grow

Book of Hours

Shelley read Rousseau in water
gathered flowers for Julie at Saint-Gengoux
floated to sea in a coracle
the last poem on foolscap sheets, stuffed in pockets
stained with salt
Rousseau's blank-eyed woman offering the cup of knowledge
his brain washed clean as sand, a final vision
Alas I kiss you Jane
her face crumpled in earth with the rest

2

Premonition

Having traveled so far you can't sleep
and nor can I such distinctions cast
in future-tense as a song without notes
a steep climb adrift in fog where stairs
peel off into dizzying sky then startled
waves of red through depths of cloud
closer still as likeness in assembly
bred gently then breathless
such kindred premonitions but you may
beg to differ already dreaming where
I no longer sleep as a fold of a rose
breeding new forms of attention
like walking while humming a song
whose words are inward in translation
then cast into a stranger's cry

Hatching

the irregular kindred body
    brims with deeds

        if burdened if possessed
          purchased wholesale

penetrable in all sentimental matters

this blank likeness
      afeast on
        eggs and salaries

          a form of ownership
          entirely unplanned

if subdivided if
sentenced

lawn fence lawn fence

what kind of eyes
in the interior

a thought breeds
      arrest   a nest
               moist and tiny bones

    hot skinned husks   homegrown
private as portions

        knock-knock   this blind lashing heart

    soft feathers and the egg tooth
    pipping

                                        hello
            you swift bride spawning
                              in flawed streets bad air

        orange and red pouring
thoroughfare

        voice another blank inside
clean and dirty city adrift
in garbage hum
                              Yes you
                darkening bruise
                        soon to be exchanged

what winged claim
                aflutter in the darkling eaves
                        cheep cheep
                                        wild tumbles and
roughshod dives

                hello nice to know you

all unborn luxuries
        priced for quick sale

this submission

          to a nest

                to debt and hurry

      a breath between ellipses
                a telling pause
thumb of pressure down the spine

                starts to feel shapely
        to encircle, a swelling thought

headfirst flung

Thirty-Ninth Month

At the cusp of Aquarius & Pisces a young hour steals through the orchard.

A passage under one slowly rotting tree.

One apple tumbles down, an overfed second yawns shut.

& the calendar spreads her legs, tears me open jaw to hip.

Pressing blind now hot unsteady.

O gaudy trespass in the split sky of waiting.

A please, an aching little pastoral unrest.

The future with its seasons still gagged & blindfolded.

O torrential downpour at winter's edge, green clamors vagrant careless & wildeyed.

Rain destroying the figs, spinach battered to shreds.

Mingling tincture of time, occulted flower, ungrown husk.

Sever & break me blood & leaking hour.

O sweep the leaves into the next storm, dark sodden spots of spring spreading.

Black seeds smashed now into flatfaced joy.

What it's like to be a _____

four-chambered thing
down on my haunches to pee
is an objective description
so he said so he said

though I was not alive
my heart beat as if a beep

hanging upside down is a
catching flies in the mouth is a
oh yes full of rich detail
a series of calculable signals
pelt brain oil womb

little palpitations & soft entrails

could reach down and in
nothing personal
fleshy yawn on flat slab
was not   was not
any matter mine

thrust inside out and splayed loose

he said colorless he said
everything just exists
a cup a purse a tube a palm

shuteyed featureless baggage
of worldly stuff
unmothered unearthed unbecoming
dear me no exchange

Habitats

Moon, nails, a cradle of pine needles
foraged from the nocturnal tree.
Pure milk flushes glass. A house as surrogate
for kindness, each beam a secret custody.
The child travelling sightless. Air
uncolored in the shallows.
Shivering now. Beeswax for warmth,
tallow, mutton fat, a keen axe.

*

The cage of water, bouncing back
a color. Gray washing and swept.
At the still center, she is using her body
wrong. Back and forth, errant.
A medicinal smell. Arms clear
a nest, light in slurred waves.

*

Greenery to crawl inside and go
soundless. Floating because motion
is common. The child's breath, a lushness
when even skin turns inward. He cannot
feel you now. The air channeled
or filling in, cool in hollowed-out
corners. What he feels is a window.

Book of Months

Uncounted weeks of winter.
If Mars is for planting and *aperire* for opening.
Named you for a god and the day sprang into belief.
Onrushing defaced the vine.
Hurtled you grassy in crushed rapture.
And Mercury's mother birthed you from a cloverleaf into the equinox.
Then the poem will steal your features like sleep.
Figs blackening in the abandoned birth canal.
Bartered lambs for your blood.
If harvest wearied you of animal gesture and the rotted sheaves of wheat.
Bones skinnied of their hoard.
Whose arms will grip you furred and suckling good night.

Theogony

Hesiod sings of all the offspring
bloody-minded and rosy
a rattle at my feet
and a strong-willed infant
who loves to grab hold, to tear

no no, not the hair, pulled
out pages from the book
sucked and spit on the carpet
at noonday after gathering fallen apples
one thuds across the floor
go slow I say as he rolls

he is mine I suppose but distant
unearthly, rattling

a song on the radio, will you wear
white oh my dear oh my dear
or who loves the sun and here's the moon
in a willow-tree
shy and fierce with force
all the dead gods eaten by fire
or thrown to sea
epic words sodden in the mouth

swollen with bee-stings
he was wrapped in a blue blanket rushed to
a room that locked me out
I woke up pounding

now he wants my face
the mothers cry out for vengeance
wailing and keening
I wear him tethered to my back
hot breath
relentless on my spine

3

Misspelled

winter in the valley
still mostly sun

how long will it last
a heart pink on yellow paper
bleeds past its border

the shape it makes
can't hold it close, can't keep still

sudden flurry of rain
steadies and drives in
goes soft, edged with rot

the boy can spell yes, no, fall
but not leaves, which do not

letters collapse into
hard roots, unearthed
what he misspells: *ran* for *rain*

For Hunger

Yesterday was nothing, empty-handed. Today was a dream, she appeared at the door with a bag of fruit she could not eat. Yesterday I was at ocean's edge and her hand ebbed from mine. To gag, to heave, to swallow deep.

A nothing full of planes and cars. One parked in the patch of roses and insisted. I measured speech in streams of escalating color. A torrent of water, loosed.

Tablecloth flung across an empty table. Sit and eat, lie down and sleep. Disowned, misremembered. Today held its breath for a long time under the current. Taught me little or left me what to say.

Today the doorbell's clamor, the wanting and wanting to turn away.

A couple of apples coated in wax and an unhappy orange. Today was a little long, bruised, still slumbering when I woke. Its eyes hooded. And the cry of someone's hunger, ungovernable.

Yesterday was a city of browning roses. Without water the thorns choke the buds. Or so I was told. Scolded. I held in warm arms and fed.

Today, children hoarding toys in the supermarket playroom. Let go, one screamed at the other. Arms tore outward like branches scratching the sky. And a distant wave broke over my eyes.

A song in hazy water, a deep-down rose languid in the hot. Twined along fences. The song bore words wakeful and mild. I was wrapped in red and granted a feast of clover.

Today the midwife, the tax collector, the father stamping in his button-down. Today twenty methods of sleep for the unquiet.

A slice of neon light in a doorway I entered in order to say, I'm hungry, or, I cannot refuse. And nothing the day is unwilling to give. A dress, a trundle bed, a plastic bag of food. Yesterday swims in yellow airless shadows, my arms reaching awkwardly up.

Salt in the rose's eye. I could not sleep so someone spoke for me. Murmurs in the aisles all crying here, a tributary of urgent colors to ignore. Fell into the nest of rock dust, blood meal, lake moss, ashes. Now shut up your gaze.

Today wanted my lungs and stomach, my circling animal mind. Today was a woman whose face I recognized, having lived inside.

Nothing brushed or mended or sewed up tight. Today a semblance, something to be said, expectant. You must eat for us both, I heard her say.

Breathless. Her voice going high and dark, nursing the solstice to the slow-swinging sea. Oh hush thee my baby the night is behind us. Swinging down to ease, to ease. From her mouth to my ear, grace.

I have not earned it, I said, though I was famished. Coughing up salt water.

Today bad weather in the lungs, a language more steadfast for its weeping, a long evening star signaling exile.

To carry the tide, a responsibility, a parcel, to be carried away, to support or bear, to carry on.

Today a debt to eat or let rot in the cupboard. Yesterday a body growing distant, earthward. To love is territory and darkness.

Yesterday an unkind surface, common as night pulled over the head.

Once I slept inside her and all her thoughts were mine. A habit of pausing for an idea to offer itself. An unexpected gift, a knock. There, a bent arm that mimics a plane passing overhead, or a door unhinged.

Hunger is reborn, as is sleep. In the dream I was eating for two. But all stories fade at the close. Today I am this house's sole occupant, its hungry embrace. What do you want, I asked the open door.

July, Late

don't think of it
                    deergrass bleached yarrow
                              what's left
                                                  in the sun
ants crawl in the poppy's eye

                                        compost tub
buckling earth scree and scrub
          wells drying up
                        weird seeds

down in the scorched grass
                    knots of sound   dark centers

                              it takes time
nothing going by

                    hard to take, no wind
in the mouth, a bitter taste

                                        stormless sky

if no one is coming
spread that shirt out to sleep on

                              no plot
no commerce, no held claim

                  hot in the ear
                                    a quite particular blue

what way not to break

                  lie still now   listen

                       something far off
a bird call

slight wind
        stirring the brush

                      a train as it moves through

Apple Cake

In the story the old woman's apron is full of plums she trades for
feathers, flowers, a gold chain, a stranger's blessing.

But I've lost it now, out the side door or slipped from a moving box.
Unseasonable rain collapses every nest and tangle, greens it then
turns it black.

The child cries out, adrift in his white sheets. Down in the valley,
valley so low, hang your head over, hear the wind blow, her old song.
Sometimes I would join in and she would stop short. Sleep now.

Woods right in the center of town. I almost hit a deer one night, driving past. He bounded out of the headlights and I held my breath for miles.

He wanted to keep running off. Apples from the cloth bag thudding onto the pavement. He cried and said, you're not mine.

In the dream I was in the dining room of the old house, eating soup while outside it snowed. She was asleep in my bed upstairs, under that pink and blue checked blanket, sweaty and sick. Clink clink went the spoon. White ice, filthy pavement. If I went up the stairs, I knew she would be gone. Taking my time, I emptied my bowl.

The name of the story is *Apple Cake*, and it turns on the question of what you are willing to lose along the way.

Here's a print of rain in the gutter. Here's a song I used to sing, the name he spells backward every time. Here's what needs repair, what's unraveled, lost its leg or wheel or button. A hand-me-down, an alphabet sung aloud, a shop closed up for the winter.

It's November, no propane in the tanks, glittery blue paper snowflakes taped in windows. Here's how you make a snow angel, he said, lying still on the rug.

The little girl on the plane screaming, "I'm here! I'm here!" and the mother murmuring, rocking her, "you're here." A child a habit, mother a promise, broken or kept.

Mommy has to work, I say, and he stands at the door each day and says, good luck! There's this buzzing in my chest, I'm grinding my teeth. Pink and soft with a mineral smell.

Another dream: she was cooking an intricate meal, anise syrup and twenty spices, Schubert on the stereo. The apartment was hers but all the colors were different.

Woke to read of the poet's death, war's red line, coffee ground very fine. Child's hair grown long, brown leaves hanging on.

He hates the winter too. "We don't say *hate*," I murmur. He hurls
the plastic boat against the window again and again, and doesn't
remember where he was last spring.

Gathered in surely as breathing, steady warmth at the nape. The
same song over and over, every night. She's just sounds in the mind.

Snow softens the ravine. Longer night, closer stars.

At story's end, the woman gets her apple cake after trading everything she has. Here's a lullaby full of doors.

Apple Core

"Man can do nothing without the make-believe
of a beginning," I underlined in the novel,
having found four apples on my mother's apple tree

the new being, after all, a blind spot,
a seed lodged in the tooth

every morning there will be singing
at the panier market

Seasonal Affective

Autumn industrial odor
               neoplastic rusty fog
nearness   neighbor she

      all circulation   all weekday traffic flood
                                 salty tea or schoolkid alley

                    kinds of rain: milky, tender, steeped, clawing
             each joy slept off
corner of birds colliding

                 only yes, more, goodbye

Crossed-off mind swarms
                                    the sea   an eyeless bomb
                    rearranging shaken
                                            always blowing in
war and ruin
                                        as if unwoven
                                                without expression

Long sleep shipwrecked
                    a wrong present try-again
            to carry forgetting
                            the tide a responsibility
                            to be carried away
                                    with debris
pure welling up
                        impenetrable voice
            but you have to try

Bad weather never yes or no
        heaves on in the lungs

                    horizontal too flimsy
      a debt unkind
                              a heavier impatience
                      is sleet and time
                            travel

a body growing distant
                          to love is

            darkness

Afterthought

it's a line I'm following
first painted white then
graphite along the edges

blue vein up the arm
or a lacy seam on a
blue dress slipped off

call it a day
great splotches of ink
tiny bits of foil

some kind of shape
in the busywork
vacuum dust fold repeat

slashed through the middle
a line flooded
in translucent black

the dark print of my hands
shadowing each task
don't leave me or let me alone

someone sleeping
in the breeze that blows
the line dry

what is made so
easily overwritten
by evening